Strange
Flesh

WILLIAM LOGAN

Strange Flesh

PENGUIN POETS

PENGUIN BOOKS
Published by the Penguin Group
Penguin Group (USA) Inc., 375 Hudson Street,
New York, New York 10014, U.S.A.
Penguin Group (Canada), 90 Eglinton Avenue East, Suite 700, Toronto,
Ontario, Canada M4P 2Y3
(a division of Pearson Penguin Canada Inc.)
Penguin Books Ltd, 80 Strand, London WC2R 0RL, England
Penguin Ireland, 25 St Stephen's Green, Dublin 2,
Ireland (a division of Penguin Books Ltd)
Penguin Group (Australia), 250 Camberwell Road,
Camberwell, Victoria 3124, Australia
(a division of Pearson Australia Group Pty Ltd)
Penguin Books India Pvt Ltd, 11 Community Centre,
Panchsheel Park, New Delhi–110 017, India
Penguin Group (NZ), 67 Apollo Drive, Rosedale, North Shore 0632,
New Zealand
(a division of Pearson New Zealand Ltd)
Penguin Books (South Africa) (Pty) Ltd, 24 Sturdee Avenue,
Rosebank, Johannesburg 2196, South Africa

Penguin Books Ltd, Registered Offices:
80 Strand, London WC2R 0RL, England

First published in Penguin Books 2008

1   3   5   7   9   10   8   6   4   2

Copyright © William Logan, 2008
All rights reserved

Page xi constitutes an extension of this copyright page.

LIBRARY OF CONGRESS CATALOGING-IN-PUBLICATION DATA
Logan, William, 1950–
Strange flesh / William Logan.
p.   cm.—(Penguin poets)
ISBN 978-0-14-311446-8
I. Title.
PS3562.O449S77   2008
811'.54—dc22   2008003514

Printed in the United States of America
Set in Goudy Old Style
Designed by Ginger Legato

for Barbara Hoffman and Rhoda Janzen

Contents

I / Homes

II / Abroads

III / Elsewheres

IV / Englands

Acknowledgments

Antioch Review: Noah; *Dark Horse*: Ballad; *Haerter* (Germany): Salon de Thé; *Hudson Review*: Bath in the Margins; Venice by the Numbers; *Kunapipi*: The Tide, 1955; *Leviathan Quarterly*: The Age of Treason; *Literary Imagination*: Wrapping Up; *Modern Review*: Joshua; *Nation*: The Blue Laws; Last Chance Saloon; *New Criterion*: Cedar Key after Storm; The Death of Ovid; The Ghost; The Tide Pool; Zero Hour; *New England Review*: The Anatomy Lesson; The Expensive Dress; The Prairie; *New Republic*: The Blessèd Redemption of Delft; The Donkey; Floods in Cambridge; *New York Sun*: London through the Glass; *New Yorker*: The Fatal Shore; *Notre Dame Review*: By the New Waters of Europe; *Paris Review*: Crossing Newfoundland; *Parnassus*: The Jubilee! The Jubilee!; *Partisan Review*: The Vision; *Poetry*: The New (Upper) Assembly Rooms; Queen Square; Song; *Salmagundi*: Christ Church, Spitalfields; The Gathering Storm; *Sewanee Review*: The Blaschkas' Invertebrates; Tenting on the Plains; *Sewanee Theological Review*: Bath; *Smartish Pace*: Venice at the Millennium; *Southern Review*: The Lost Boy; *Southwest Review*: Girl with a Pearl Earring; *TLS*: Argument (as part of Magpie); The Beast in the Jungle; The Farm; The Luxembourg Gardens; Magpie; Mocha Dick; *32 Poems*: Hometown; Paris in Winter; *Virginia Quarterly Review*: Dante's Folly; Untitled in Four Parts; *Warwick Review*: The Manger; *Washington Square*: 1923; *Yale Review*: Amsterdam; Dawn Chorus.

Strange
Flesh

For there is a poetry in wildness, and every
alligator basking in the slime is in himself an Epic,
self-contained.

—*Martin Chuzzlewit*

Homes

The Death of Ovid

Arched trees flare against the early leaf.
Over the spent horizon, like a scrawl,
gold clouds have worked a naked bas-relief.
The smoke of raging fires casts a pall.

The Fatal Shore

The horseshoe crab in frail armor-plate,
broken open as if by a javelin throw,
lay in the sand like a cracked jam-jar,
the son of some Trojan.

Achilles, too, arrived *in medias res*
at his mortal scene.
The booming foghorn, the groaning buoy,
tide by tide by tide

kept their mockeries to themselves.
Was there no end to them?
Lost Renaissance studies with a sepia cast,
the dunes receded in perspective.

Fog lounged in the marsh shallows.
A soda-colored dawn again and again
rubbed salt into the clapboards,
collapsing upon a radiant wild-eyed dailiness.

Dullness, too, was my god.
Tangled knobs of seaweed
drifted up the beach on the curt tide,
like Myrmidons out of work.

The Ghost

The shabby, dishonored, unnamed ghost
who haunted my parents' dream life like a guest

must have been, I realized thirty years late,
my father's alcoholic father, who, light

on his feet, jitterbugged through my Pittsburgh childhood
with debts, girlfriends, his leathery moods—

a figure beyond our suburban world.
When his car roared up, my mother curled

her upper lip—not that we cared, glad for his hoarse
attentions, his growl-laugh, the source,

I know now, of my father's apish guffaws.
Why didn't we see Grandfather's flaws,

the headaches that kept him in bed, weekend mornings,
his lack of a job? There must have been other warnings;

and yet we were too young for the secrets slurred
in every sentence, almost every word.

Only once, I recall, did we visit *him*.
Somewhere in Ohio, caretaker at a nursing home—

no, a funeral parlor! A third wife vaguely in attendance.
(They lived, perhaps, upstairs?) The memories make no sense,

not that it matters; but, without his failings,
would my father's life have been plain sailing?

They were both drawn, despite a lack of guile,
to the trumpeting, sad world of sales,

where, one wounded summer, as if into my inheritance,
I walked our suburb's rackety fences,

trying to peddle steak knives, carving knives,
to wary, bewildered, perfumed wives.

My father saw my discouragement, then despair,
and rescued me from it. Life is not fair.

Why, now, recall the vain, bearlike man
who, one winter morning, waltzed into the kitchen

to demand breakfast from my mother, and perhaps more,
though he had died three years before?

It took the rest of her life to settle the score.

The Farm

Fireflies took the fields like sparks,
the hay fumes rising in the half-light.
Even in the dream, something seemed wrong.
A creak in the hayloft, an old scythe

rusting on its hook, a whinny from a broken stall.
Manure I should have shoveled at dusk,
the lopsided sack of oats, but also something other.
I closed the barn and walked to the house,

where the screen door squeaked, not unmusically.
Each splintered stair offered its private complaint.
I climbed past the framed photographs,
our ancestors fragile and grim even in youth,

and opened the door to the bedroom.
My mother lay there, windows open,
lace curtains spreading and closing
with the wave of an invisible hand.

The kerosene lamp had gone out.
There was a ragged Bible in this dream,
open to Isaiah. Somehow I knew it was Isaiah.
A softened burr rattled the window screen . . .

a house wasp battering to get out.
I thought, *Oh, no, not yet. Not yet.*

The Tide Pool

The name of the town is lost.
A Kodak memory
restores the glacial scree
our bored Atlantic crossed

that burning July day.
The crowded tide drove in
like a release of sin
along the rocky bay,

leaving scattered tide pools
abandoned in its wake.
Beneath the glazed opaque
surface swam dark schools

that thrashed in private wars.
The pools were a modest hell—
a crab with a broken shell,
a starfish showing its scars.

Under the water-glass,
the fragile creatures wavered
as if a god had favored
their untidy, cramped crevasse,

though one by one
the infant pools dried.
The weaker creatures died
beneath a cursory sun.

I saw that blinding wave
once more, beating the glacial rocks
below the broken docks,
when I stood at your grave.

Mocha Dick

The humpbacked lawyer lay on the sand,
figure of mystery and uncanny gift—
what did we think, we children of the shore,
as the sun rose like a headlamp?

The Victorians who settled the Horseneck
lay curing beneath the Geodetic Survey's brass mark
in the Methodist cemetery.
We owed them manners and our solvent despairs.

The beach houses once swanky as Newport's,
wind scarred, imperious, stared down
their enemy, Melville's coarse, brute sea
battering the sand with its bull's head.

Like a sperm whale. Like Mocha Dick.
Here and there a scandalous chimney leaned
into my vacant and unseasoned boyhood.
The lighthouse swung its beam

back and forth like a mace.

The Manger

The cruel, uneven dawn
grayed to a sponge-painted wall.
At eleven, I wanted to own
the corroded, omnipotent gods.

How insignificant they looked,
Sunday breakfasts
when I gorged their bread and wine.
The brassy cross shimmered from a catalogue;

the cassocks and carpets were canonical.
I used to page the hymnal
like a criminal,
recalling the ingenious sufferings

of each ready-made saint.
Our priest dragged out a life-size manger—
Joseph's aquiline nose chipped away,
and the measly, helpless child staring up

at the nothing that is nothing.

Cedar Key after Storm

The fish shacks turned an oystery glow,
the drowned light more intense.
Along the blank sky low
clouds learned from experience.

A bridge leapt over the inlet
where sawtooth reeds had bedded,
like spears in rusting silhouette,
as the summer storm receded.

Carved from gray blocks of wood,
enormous sad pelicans
on the concrete balustrade stood
stiff as librarians,

as if they dimly knew
the mighty events to come.
The distant thunder grew
fainter, like a brushed kettle-drum.

And you were a great bird, sickly,
fleeing the northern weather.
Ten years had passed quickly
since we watched the gulf together.

Look back now at the theft
of boredom, and jazz, and the rages,
and see what little is left—
just a book of the thinnest pages.

Your voice was the gentlest whisper,
your health had gone so fast.
Of all the things you were,
perhaps that would be the last.

i.m. Donald Justice (1925–2004)

The Lost Boy

He seemed no more than a character
from the pages of a Hardy novel.
Where was his soul, flickering through the dunes?

The sea's night-foil glittered.
In yellow slickers, men from the town
blasted their yacht foghorns

like beaters at the hunt.
Knotted with bayberry and Masonic
wisdom, the unfenced dunes blazed

like clotted cream.
Anxious gulls swooped in wrecked flourishes.
I saw the boy through a crack in my windowpane,

his chest bared like the dead Chatterton's.
The ironclad horseshoe crabs
scrabbled along the tide line,

as if finishing their autobiographies.
Like travelers on holiday,
tides penned their regrets twice a day.

Untitled in Four Parts

i.

Dawn boils up like milk, cloudy with disrespect.
Like Tin Pan Alley hacks, paid for each line,
neighborhood wrens bang out their high-pitched notes.
The narrow windows offer nothing, the glass
brushed with dark leaf-shapes, like a Japanese scroll.
A smudge of nimbus glows. The gray burns to blue.
Love is now overrated, out of date—
when I first glimpsed you in those palm-frond days,
my heart consoled itself in heats of longing.
Your creamy flesh has chipped away like marble,
your ink-black hair filling with silver vein.
Time's furnaces are banked, the wood yards gone.
Downriver something steams, two plumes of smoke,
with fire belching from its barren stacks.

ii.

Adam in his frame, Eve at last in hers.
Having no words, they must make empty signs.
How do we know, how do we know the sign?
The girl in the pale albumen photograph
takes off her dress and stares back. There it is,
the magpie poignance of the stolen life.
Upstairs a something stirs within the womb,
and downstairs griping mourners grip the corpse,
bearing the ruined heaven in its weight.
The vision in the photograph says nothing,

only the *there* that needed to be said.
In Cranach's diptych, the couple hesitates—
drawing the thorny leaves across their skin,
divided from each other by their shame.

iii.

How many stumbled in Sodom's painted halls
or greeted death below Gomorrah's stairs?
The grain of new experiment rubs away.
Urbs turn to suburbs, naked, garish, endless,
the Renaissance perspective doomed to grace
where each tarred footprint knows the path to God.
The ordered trees, scorched clean of mockingbirds,
waver in nervous ranks like smooth-cheeked sentries,
recruited in the provinces, stuck in Rome
without the language or the will to pain,
just hanging on till the hills are set alight
or traitorous flocks of cranes come home to roost.
Feathered barbarians kneel at the gates.
All for a paycheck, some acres free and clear.

iv.

The mists leak cream, clouds filthier than cream,
dragged like an afterthought from the sky's lead bowl.
Redemptive hills march toward the fallen sea.
In this uncertain spring, the lilacs blaze

like Deco chandeliers. Seasick with hope,
each dawn Odysseus casts off for home
with ten years on his watch. Is Nausicaa
a snapshot now, crossed through in his black book?
What guard dog answers at the old address?
By dawn the wren has spent itself in song,
a file rasped against a bicycle chain.
Greeting the mirror, I cannot recognize
the gray-haired revenant grown picket boned,
the stranger's bitter glance like rotten wood.

The Tide, 1955

Romanticism . . . is dangerously lighted
by those bayonets that Blake and Goethe
observed passing their garden hedges.

—George Steiner

The passion has drained slowly, like the tide.
In the watery haze, a bored girl contemplates
the languor of the anemone's arms,
the clever crab with its torn claw—

and in everything the taste of salt.
A freighter perches on the horizon like a finial.
The dead are old news. The last war seethes
on the sailor's forearms. Each hour

passes the eye in downward flight.

Hometown

How does a river grow older?
The houses gleamed like silver salt-boxes,
ready to be shaken by a giant.
This was the town of fish—in every cottage,

a swordfish sword rusted over the mantle.
The whalers' clapboards were capped by widow's walks.
Fishing boats huddled together for winter,
grumbling quietly to themselves.

The dusty main road snaked down a hill
to the wharves, then turned around,
as if unsure where to go—it could
only go back again, as if in embarrassment.

The town seemed to be dreaming.
There lay the two-room schoolhouse, out of work.
There our old house, a half-size version of itself,
crouched behind its crumpled stone wall

and twelve untidy rosebushes.
Our not-so-stately maple had been cut down.
On the edge of town stood an abandoned drive-in,
parking lot crammed with rusting machinery,

like toys abandoned by the giant's baby.

The Prairie

The winding road beneath the ancient oaks,
edged with palmetto scrub, like nature's little jokes,

cut a crooked path to that antique Eden,
one that God forgot. A place like Sweden.

Past the sudsy gray lake where water boiled,
the treeless, marshy prairie, still unspoiled,

unfolded to the horizon, a hand-drawn chart
with monsters at the corners, like a work of art.

We lay beneath the gray-green oaks to rest,
while blizzards rang their changes further west.

Then, before us, a red-shouldered hawk
dropped like the hand of an invisible clock

into dry cracked reeds. The day grew still,
as if someone somewhere had grown ill.

At last the hawk lifted, with something in its claws—
even Dame Nature has unkind laws.

And that was all. No one else was there to see,
or provide the consolation of philosophy.

When we turned back, the breeze had shifted,
or was that cloud like an eyebrow lifted?

Dante's Folly

The atmosphere of Newton's elaboratory,
like a world within a wood. Amid gross weeds,
the steamy incense cured the censor tongue
blazing out fire scarcely night or day.
Page by galled page, the faint deliberate
monsters grew new and mathematical.
Nocturnal insects climbed the looser stars,
and even moths betrayed intelligence,
aware that *chymical* experiments
drew purgatory in the fall of tides.
The heron's pantheistic trinity
chewed on the dry moon's philosophic wobble.
Hell marshes waited, green with theology,
the alligator's cross and passioned eye.

Wrapping Up

Each visit I was surprised to find her alive,
like a queen within the ruin of her hive.

She swanned into the room, after hours of preparation,
as if some foreign prince were waiting at the station,

then stared out over the glittering coins of river,
her olive eyes just moving. It made me shiver.

A line of makeup wavered across her brow,
like the tidemark on some broken scow.

It was easy to forget that men had once adored her.
Above, her skin was pale—the disputed border

where a great war had been fought, or a neighborhood spat,
or where she'd just removed an invisible hat.

Her cold face was crazed like onionskin,
legs now turkey bones, she'd grown so thin.

We offered each dusty object on a tray.
She nodded, smiling gloomily—*I'm not myself today*—

but turned her fist, thumb up or down,
like Caligula. She managed a seductive frown,

sending fragments of her old life to their doom,
knowing in the end we must clear the room.

Some things had been in storage twenty years,
yet still she greeted each with pretty tears,

as if it were *she* who was to blame.
Who was that man? she asked. *I can't recall his name.*

He's dead . . . I think. Not much use, this.
I threw away some ceramic cows. It was a kind of bliss

to pack her life into each cardboard box—
Victorian whatnots, three unsprung clocks.

We children were cold suburban Fates,
known by our less-attractive traits.

I'm slow today, she said. *Are you sure you don't mind?*
Was she worried by what secrets we might find?

There *wasn't* one, not really, though in her mothballed sweaters
lay a grimy, ribboned packet of letters

from some first sergeant who might have married her.
That must have been the last of her *cris de coeur.*

She turned on us, with the thinnest smile,
as if she hadn't seen us the whole while,

as if that's how the end of life must seem,
as if she'd just had the oddest dream.

Zero Hour

Bittern, hawk, and osprey tend
     in their private circles near
orders scrawled across the page,
though the willing victims send
postcards to another age
     gazing up in fear.

Alligators known to dwell
     in the analytic root
theorize about the will.
Bureaucrats consign to hell
inconvenient villains still
     prepared to shoot.

Will indignant vultures perch,
     waiting for the halt and weak
on whose bounty they descend?
In a large and vacant church,
words whose meanings some defend
     have yet to speak.

II

Abroads

Argument

You measured the cold field like a ghost.
Out in the raw Atlantic,
the freighters anchored, not the least romantic.
New storms stood building off the coast.

Crossing Newfoundland

First appear the tiniest islands, crumbs
brushed off the mainland, each outlined
in Chinese white, as if by a child. The islands
trail cartoon white wisps, to show they're moving.
Then come shards crazed by dark veins,
Verde Alpi on faded blue tablecloth.
Look closer. You can see the threads of rivers,
pale green valleys like lichen inching across a wall.
Who might be walking there? No one we know.
No one we need to know. Then land
and more land, pocked by meteorites,
sometimes with the faintest blush of pink
or, in the crevices, a dusting of snow.
Why is that valley speckled orange, the one
near the lopsided lake? Is that an alluvial plain?
It's clear as an illustration in a geography book.
Doesn't the lake with the umbilical cord
look like a manta ray? A religious people
lie on lawns and find shapes in clouds,
but the view from the sky is a scientist's.
The traveler's curiosity is the same
as a god's, somehow above it all.
Look! Those patches of shagreen must be trees;
and I can spy, the cabin window
my magnifying glass, tall pines abandoned
in the middle of a river, a lonely island,
a lake half silted—the silt is the shadow.
That mountain is frosted like a Bundt cake.
What expeditions we might make!
What valleys and canyons we might name

after ourselves! What miniature countries
we might discover, or dream of discovering!
But now the clouds have closed again,
like curtains on an old, often-rehearsed play.

Girl with a Pearl Earring

In The Hague, Den Haag, the shop
that flogs law books
offers a set of dinner plates
with a justice's black robe on the rim.

Crisis = opportunity.
Opportunity = profit.
Profit = justice.
The Rights of Man has been slashed

to a price anyone can afford.
We shivered as the Mauritshuis cracked its doors.
There she hung, in an unheated room,
a seventeenth-century movie star,

Vermeer's *Girl with a Pearl Earring.*
A world glowered in that opalescence—
just, according to scholars,
a bulb of blown glass

lined with ground fish-scales.
She stared at *A View of Delft*
in her dreamy, stunned, adolescent way—
calculating, a Jonathan Edwards.

In Vermeer's vision of Renaissance order,
each brick had been mortared
in its proper universe.
To reconcile the eye, he wrestled

the city gate toward the viewer
and wrenched old churches
off their foundations.
You can stand by the highway and judge for yourself.

The Anatomy Lesson

Desiring one angelic portrait of the dead,
and having at hand only the accoutrements
of their trade, and knowing it was winter,
they laid out the corpse for a painter
whose work they admired for his butcher's
knowledge of dead game and his scientific hand
at flowers. The body opened like a rose,
late bloom resisting the advance of season,
though legally they were constrained, the anatomists,
to dissect only a hanged man. The shroud
would henceforth be his armored nakedness,
his skin the execution of paint. Surrounded
by the woolens of Calvinist finery,
the violated corpse seemed the more naked,
open to the folios of Galen and Vesalius,
walls glowing in the soul-like flicker
of scented candles fending off the agreeable
stench of decay. The painter hurried to perfect
this portrait of what, after all, proved a mystery
of the soul. He could have laid down
the *memento mori* of the skull, the candle,
the crawling caterpillar; but it was perhaps
more pointed to make the anatomists themselves
like corpses, silent in the house of William
the Silent, like words about to be spoken.

Amsterdam

Rembrandt was nearer to us.
Along the green canals, oozing
with wounded stonework,
cold as July was spotlit, a smell

pursued the seventeenth century,
last chance for the painter to free
what was buried in the paint.
The gables were cut from paper,

moss steaming on cracked slates.
A flight of pigeons wheeled
like a defeated army
returning again and again

to colonize the sedated empire
of our mistakes.
Not that we ceased to make them.
You stood in a dented halo of light

on the central square, where drug dealers
with the confidence of stockbrokers
had staked out a monument.
Trust was the watchword,

cash the medium of betrayal.
You took me as I lounged by the dark canal,
my one long-haired photograph.
You were dead five years before I heard.

i.m. SUZI MOORE (1949–1995)

The Blessèd Redemption of Delft

Rank with the clotted, simmering greens,
the sleek canals were overgrown
with shade, and then the thought of shade
   the painter made his own.

The rain was taught by harder rains,
as if the heavens disagreed
with that distinguished, apostolic light
   consoling in its need.

He loved the century's moral itch,
the mortal purpose of the eye,
revealing what would constitute
   a civilized reply.

Within the burnished, gilded frame,
the oil starts to turn to flesh,
as if the burning of long silences
   let us begin afresh.

       I.M. CAREL FABRITIUS (1622–1654)

Salon de Thé

The waiters at the *salon de thé* moved
into the memory of elegance.
The false orange trees in the orangerie

swayed with the divinity
Eve was given, afflicted with the choice
of a miniature evolution of the soul.

On the tray before us,
the *petits fours* and *tartes au citron*
carried back the ardors of a sullied universe

beneath the downward flocks of pigeons
pinned to the obelisk in the Place de la Concorde.
On the hills of Darjeeling, the first flush

of the tea bushes exfoliated in a drowse.
The burnished air measured an instinct for arrival.
We had come nearly to the end,

pilgrims whose pilgrimages were mistaken.

Paris in Winter

The *bateaux* still ply the opaque Seine,
the water green as mold.
Tourist boats, laid up by the quays,
in summer waddle downriver

shimmering like glass houses.
In the shadows, you can see
the ruins of the Roman city,
its silent order bedded

in philosophy. Beneath the Cluny,
the baths shine like an excavated skull,
emptied of the pliancy of the human.
Roof slates like fish scales burn across the river.

At Christmas, headless angels,
stuffed with kapok, float above the digital
notice boards in Notre Dame.
When the flashbulbs pop,

everyone glares like a messiah,
like Mantegna's arrow-
spitted St. Sebastian—
martyr, porcupine.

The Luxembourg Gardens

It was dawn as I walked
through the Luxembourg Gardens,
the dawn of Christmas Eve,
when even hope runs thin.

Ice lay on the fountain
like a sheet of tin,
and across it a gull
dragged something awful,

something beyond pardon.
The silhouettes of trees
rose through the lacquered air
above the classical terrace

where twelve naked Galateas,
their marble skin powdery and dull,
stood frozen to death.
The iron garden-chairs were scattered,

as if a party had just ended
and the guests rushed away.
Beyond the pollarded chestnuts
and Medici fountain,

the ghosts of innocents played.

Venice at the Millennium

It's too unlikely to be real, you said,
as the ghostly voyaging hulk
of S. Giorgio Maggiore
rose foggily from the lagoon.

March tides lapped the stones
of the Piazzetta. Wafers of water
crept forward, crept back, back,
until we lay unconscious once more

beneath the fresco of a down-
at-heels pensione. It was still the dawn
of the Reagan administration.
Gods coupled with gods

across the cracks in the ceiling.
Lizards crossed the red-tiled roofs
into their own belittled country,
plotting revolution.

By night the *acqua alta* nipped our heels.
The pensione's *bella donna*
slumped in her widow's weeds,
napping by the oriel window,

the city fresh with the stink
of slaughtered fish.
Or was that just the ocean
scheming to regain lost ground?

Venice by the Numbers

Glaring from a shop window,
the varnished reproductions of Canaletto
looked like the real thing.
Our guide flushed pink, as if undercooked.

You left your camera on the steps
of Ca' Rezzonico, as if you couldn't bear
reminder of poor Mrs. Browning
and her spaniels. Around every corner

lay Marco Polo's litter-strewn courtyard,
Byron's peeling coffeehouse,
or merely a boarded-up church
under restoration until . . . the date

had been weathered away.
We were under restoration ourselves.
Part of a life later, my beloved nonwife,
we found the walls inside that church

marbled with offcuts of Roman columns,
liverish, cream,
like cross sections of vital organs.
The city had sunk another half inch,

yet things refused to change.
Across the Grand Canal,
Mercury danced the Charleston above,
while Atlas held the world in his arms.

Elsewheres

Joshua

The hawks' pitched cries
woke the leaves to motion,
though the sun had paused
like a searchlight over the ocean.

Ballad

The street of cookware lies
at the base of Crockery Hill,
where the poor go down for money
and the rich go down for the thrill.

The light-skinned girls are handsome,
standing out of the light,
but the husky, sloe-eyed beauties
shave their cheeks at night.

O say where you bought the orchid
wilting in your hair,
and where the scar on your eyelid,
and where, O where, O where.

For the day is charged on credit
and the night unspent like milk,
and nobody escapes them,
and nobody lies on silk.

> *O do not cry in the grottoes,*
> *O do not mourn for the deep,*
> *for the dead will never love us*
> *and the living are asleep.*

Now Johnny washed dirty glasses
at the local tapas bar,
and Frankie was a rich girl
in a red Mercedes car.

His eye stared like a bandage.
She had the solemn face
of a stone Anaximander
on the walls of Samothrace.

The words unsaid between them
are what we cannot know,
like the anxious cry of static
on a transistor radio.

O where are the chaste who sugar
the bitter unsweetened tea,
and where the salary packet,
and where the salary?

> *O mourn for the twisted flatware,*
> *O weep for the lost caress*
> *where the fish swim by in silence*
> *and the sheets give a false address.*

They found Johnny's naked body
beneath the Bridge of Sighs
among the little fishes
that tell outrageous lies.

Frankie walked to the courtroom
and kissed the judge on the cheek,
but he frowned and gave her a sentence
of a year and a day and a week.

The months flew off like angels
on their way to a year and a day;
but the week passed all too slowly,
and they sent her on her way.

O do not say you love me,
O do not say again
that the lies are white like paper
and the truth a fountain pen.

1923

She was a faceless child then,
at a faceless boarding school,
just seven or eight when her mother
sailed for Spain one blue November morning

and vanished. Letters were returned
unopened. The children were shipped
to some sort of home in Norfolk.
They didn't have a father—he'd been confined

to an institution after the Armistice.
They were marched to a locked room,
where a shock-haired old woman
drew from her skirt a rusty iron key.

Behind that door, she said,
lay the mummified remains of a baby,
still on the table where it was born,
a baby without a mother, and if they were bad . . .

When the girl read *Great Expectations*,
she came to believe the locked room
preserved the remains of Miss Havisham's
wedding breakfast, down

to the ruined cake, gnawed by mice.
And on the table the parchment-faced baby.
Two years later, their mother returned,
her skin like crumbling chalk.

She never spoke about the missing years.
Perhaps she'd been mixed up in something
political. Things went back to normal,
or the normal that children have to call normal.

The Blue Laws

My mother, a brunette, hurried in her cloth coat
through postwar Sundays that fell

as they were meant to fall, too slowly.
Hair windblown, laddered nylons askew,

she leaned against a Packard
to straighten a seam. They were young,

my parents, nursing their rusty prewar love,
though that was never again the love they had survived.

Having seen all and said nothing, there he slouched
at the back of the lecture room, my father,

a sailor on the GI Bill, with his outdated jacket
and navy slang. He tottered on his new land legs,

his eyes wearing that seagoing barnacle-stare.
Every Sunday my mother stole off to the city

to drink illegally, until silent and sick.
And then in its way the war was over.

Song

The seduction of force comes from below.

—Simone Weil

One, two, three o'clock, then you go.
Clocks move fast, but time moves slow.
I thought I knew, but I don't know.

The countries quarrel, to and fro.
It's darker out and starting to snow.
You promised yes but then said no.

Without the bombs, the crops don't grow.
The market sank to an all-time low.
If you don't love me, just say so.

The Beast in the Jungle

i.

Met a girl at a party, beautiful girl. And I go, *Hey! We meet, like, in Rome?*
And she goes, *No way. You were that guy in Naples, waiting, waiting for something.*

ii.

So we wait. She's thirty, I'm thirty-five. Then she's sixty, I'm sixty-five. So she goes, *Hey, I'm gonna die.*
And I go, *No way.*
And she goes, *You see that thing yet, that tiger or whatever?*
And I go, *Nope.*
And she goes, *That's what you think.*

iii.

So she dies, and someone else gets all her money. I go away for, like, a year. See Asia. Then I come back. I go see her grave. And I think, like, *Shit, I should have married her.*

The Vision

They didn't know just why they had been chosen—
by whom or what would always be unclear.
That night the last remains of hope were frozen
into the consolation of their fear.

The spirit falters when the vision dies,
knowing the shapes in darkness that appall.
Around the garden rose the famous cries
of crows: *Awe, awe, awe, awe.* Then came the Fall.

A colder evening, then a bitter dawn.
The silence dropping on them like a sheet
composed a scene in which the light had drawn
a scribbled figure in the empty street.
They knew a little of oblivion,
the force in things that makes a thing repeat.

Last Chance Saloon

You were lying next to me; then it was a decade later.
The skies were awash with gray, one shade
sliding over another like a television signal,

and the years, fodder for cattle bellowing
on the common. They changed their spots
as the seasons parted, the apples

falling like experiments in textbook physics.
I heard your name on the television
and swiveled around, but it was an actress

with an automatic. She muffled her lines,
and she had an attitude. It was too cold to snow—
the television's black-and-white skies

hung like a line of old washcloths.
Remember those westerns with their Last Chance Saloons,
always in the town of Dry Gulch?

That was in another country,
where we thought we had salvaged our ideals
if we did active harm rather than passive kindness.

Noah

That great false Texas sky, the color of oatmeal,
wrapped the homely town like a blanket.
Rain had greened the range grass like spring—

even the locals were confused. Was it a sign?
The grasshoppers had gone all peculiar again.
We passed a yard that had two of everything:

two motorless pickup trucks, two washing machines,
two oil pumps frozen in attitudes of despair,
even two dogs that struck and quarreled like wolves.

Tenting on the Plains

> We bade good-by to railroads at Louisville.
>
> —ELIZABETH CUSTER

i. By Steamer to New Orleans

The steamer bumped the hooded shore,
lost paradise of hickory and sycamore,
and Negroes appeared, in quilted pants,
running across the gangplank like ants.

One toppled in. I imagined a devil's toll
at every wood lading, some ragged soul
swept under the boat to eternity.
The general pretended to be sorry for me.

Sometimes at night the great pine torches,
like resinous knots burning on porches,
made a weird and gruesome sight.
We walked the deck in artificial moonlight

and saw one plantation after another drowned,
the noble houses fallen, stark, uncrowned,
into cold abandoned lakes of water,
while ramshackle barn and slave quarter

floated out of sight. Sometimes the cows
huddled on a wart of hill, in stiff-necked rows,
helplessness and pity on their faces.
I wished the battles had been fought in desert places.

ii. Mrs. Custer in Texas

Six months afterward
(my complexion hopelessly thickened
and darkened), my poor indignant mother looked
        at that last unpardonable crime,
            my face. Swollen with sunburn,
almost parboiled, I caught myself in the glass.

He'd never cast me
    out, my husband whispered, though I turn
black as a Negro. We were the first Yankees,
        sakes!, dirt Texans ever saw. Though rich,
            some of them lived in cabins,
filthy as white trash. Dressed lumber from the gulf

        cost a ransom then—
    rough logs, unpainted, were all rude wealth
could afford; and yet they played a piano
        and laid out glass and Irish linen.
            The local alligators
were quite as partial to babies as to blacks.

        Did they taste as good?
    When our column marched, the Negroes sat
on fences like a row of polite black crows.
        We asked questions no soul could answer.
            What color is a pale horse?
How soon is ten, no, twenty miles down the road?

We foraged at farms
till we'd mustered a turkey a week.
Our cook, who owned the most arcane collection
of Negro oaths, would seize the great bird
and wring its tough skinny neck
while mumbling something unintelligible.

He'd been a preacher,
my maid Eliza claimed. Believing
each scrawny Texas fowl owned a mortal soul,
he gave each of them funeral rites.
Imagine! The general
and I nearly smothered ourselves in laughter.

iii. Dakota Territory, Spring, 1873

We came unprepared for bad weather,
renting a half-built cabin
lacking fireplace or cook stove,
alone on the unfinished prairie.

Snow fell the first night,
kept falling, slipping through cracks
onto the counterpane, where the general lay ill.
It gathered, fluffy as new wool.

I nibbled the crusts of sandwiches
packed from the train. Past midnight,

something banged the narrow door—
half-a-dozen soldiers

who had seen a candle through the glass.
There was no bedding to offer, just carpets
sewn up in bundles. We spread them out
and rolled up a soldier in each,

their feet and fingers hard with frostbite,
letting the poor boys drink, over the objections
of the cook, a bottle of alcohol
meant for the spirit lamps.

The drifts had risen to the upper windows.
Only one of the servants was of much use—
the other twisted himself into an icy corner
and would not move. A drove of stray mules

battered the clapboard walls, kicking
and braying, then vanished into the blankness.
I saw the general's favorite horse—the poor beast!—
stare longingly through our frosted window,

but when I opened the door it was gone.
We had almost fallen into a frozen sleep
when a pack of hogs, maddened with the cold,
hammered at the walls again and again,

trying to tip over the frail cabin.
They wailed like infants, like something out of hell.
It was beyond bearing.
Then another hour, another, another,

until the alien sun burned across the snow.

IV

Englands

Magpie

The magpie strutted the new lawn,
clipped and groomed as if in death.
Such are the revenants of the heath,
the bird at attention like a boxwood pawn.

Queen Square

We were the only Americans in Bath,
the hotel porter claimed, kicking our bags.
A carpenter drilled holes through the wainscotting,
exposing the eighteenth-century brick.

Beyond the revolving door of the hotel
the obelisk wavered, reduced by lightning
to half its height. Our only job was to spend money.
We paced the hills with their geometry lessons—

the square, the circle, finally the crescent—
Georgian development at a Georgian pace
by architects who amused themselves first,
then their clients. As in Jane Austen,

everyone was for sale—her costumes were hawked
outside the Jane Austen Centre, her face
shilling the chocolates, tea towels,
gilt silhouettes, the bars of soap.

Down the green and hesitant valley,
its mist laid on by a watercolorist in a hurry,
the tidy villages stood widowed,
unviolated except by the A36.

Civil servants had smudged the hillsides,
then offered subsidies for morris dancing.
Out of season, too proud to eat gleanings,
ring-necked pheasants mounted the fence posts.

Bath

How the sunlight loved the stone.
Dawn pricked each Palladian window,
each fussy wreath, each lyre, each Gorgon.

The Georgian doorways stood immune to fashion,
marching down the hill like a phalanx
toward the local cathedral, where soldiers

in stone still fought the War of 1812.
Light burned the limestone,
as if it had righted itself above the ancient hot springs.

Discreet signs warned us not to touch the water.
In the Pump Room, tea came
with a sour glass of it—sterilized, heated,

dribbling from the mouth of a stone trout.
Even the waiter had never taken a sip.
His hair stood up as if electrified.

Steam floated above the waters like a crown.

The New (Upper) Assembly Rooms

Behind the scenes,
the great marble columns of the Assembly Rooms
(see *Northanger Abbey*, chapter 2)
proved just plaster and wood.

A ragged hole in a pedestal
might have been gnawed by a Regency mouse.
In the basement, the historical dresses,
dehumidified, protected by beetle traps,

five centuries of gowns and undergarments,
the seen and not meant to be seen,
hung on gesso mannequins, like one
of the brassy-blonde twenties fortune-huntress

who married a maharaja. The poorly dressed
applauded her beaded French sheaths.
The silk of Spitalfields weavers
still embraced its sheen, though Huguenot

Protestantism lies on the scrap heap.
Where a man's fortune once turned
on the fall of cards, the rooms had been gutted,
repainted in Klee's colors of heritage,

darker in these winter days
so short they prefer not to be numbered.
What is more precious than stone,
if it last through Baedeker raids

and the high explosive of modern architecture?

Bath in the Margins

A reliquary glint consoles the stone,
as if the city had been laid in mothballs.
The quarried limestone breaks the patent light
in Georgian orders, close-ranked ornaments

drifting down crescent and circus like a dream.
King George's madness fired the Roman walls—
the headlong, puffed-up, steamy clinch of empire
cost the king's enterprise its dreaming spires,

the lost battalions, the mutiny, the poor.
Regency costume bought its backdrops cheap.
The cannon spiked upon the merchant's tomb
rusted into a monument. The baths

slumbered a hundred years, a thousand, waking
to dot-com empires. Sulphurous vinegar
spews from the tap—the taste liverish,
clipped pewter on the tongue. Forgive the dead,

whose monsters live in mirrors of the soul.
Over the seashell pallor of cold stone,
wind blackens the frayed outline of the peaks,
as if the state had touched them with a finger.

London through the Glass

The skyline of London unfolded
a fogbound map, the air frayed
as gaslight. On the discarded napkin,
I drew a rotunda—lopsided,

the debased heir of Wren's
confident scribbles,
of which almost half are left,
churches that rose from the ashes

of the Great Fire. The city
was a low jumble from which their quills
trembled, spires
pointing accusing fingers.

The buildings have grown taller,
their knowledge of God less theological.
Across the river the London Eye
revolved almost imperceptibly,

the eye of opportunity.
Great cities were built
on the commerce of ashes.
We looked into the past and blinked.

By the New Waters of Europe

i. England, That England

The poplars blackened, as if from rot,
against the gray of Constable's sky,
graduating down toward dampened pinks,
like the flush of a woman's parts.

They appeared, the trees, a pierced silhouette,
ghosts, revenants, the bemedaled, wounded reserves
marching to the front that recedes, recedes,
a tide retreating from the flat shore.

New broods of swifts tested their wings
and whistled at dusk from the hunger.
We knew what awaited them, we who were
wise before our time and now were wise after.

ii. History Lesson

The moon is down. The distant sound of lead
takes nothing but the privacy of the slain,
the fretfulness of leaves, the reasoned rain,
the nothing that is nothing when it's said.

iii. German Hours

I had been unconscious. The reflecting pool
rustled like a strip of cellophane,
and the uncertain sky shivered, a pail
of water in which God picked up his cell phone.

How beautiful you were, nevertheless,
leaning over me like a damaged angel,
knowing but not caring for the loss
of what we were, for which we fell.

The Gathering Storm

Black clouds draped the buildings like a shroud
there in the close distance, where North Sea gulls
took the wintry pickings of the town.
Each morning on the common,

they dragged the sea ashore, seeking
the consolation of empty ground.
The grass was almost gilded there, flecked
with tithes of light—stored up, reckoned,

disposed as if to the poor, extinguished.
The cracked windows caught what light was left,
dusk cranking forward on its interminable ratchet.
The wrecked graveyard courted the Victorian shadow.

There was no way back and one way forward
into that Old World, pre-world panic.
The storm drew its heavy curtains
over the river's corroded arches,

the Barnack stone turning gold to dun
over seven mute swans and one intruder,
a black Australian—transplanted, banished, a sore thumb.
And yet nothing in the scene seemed wrong.

The Donkey

A donkey lived along that river,
penned into a brick garden, the walls
flaring like disease—chalk pitted, snowflaked
with lichen, blooming in verdigris.

You could hear him braying
where swans brooded below the abandoned
houseboat, sunk in the cold mapled shadows
of the weir. The philosophers

trudging their dusty stoa,
exchanging notions of the moral life—
you could hear them a long way downriver, too,
the river of history, where battles are lost,

innocent children gutted, boundaries shifted
by a peace commission of bearded scoundrels
who hand over a few trunks of gold bangles
or the head of a luckless general.

Years later, as we walked the towpath again,
the gates of the hidden garden stood open.
I don't remember if the house had fallen
into ruin—it stood alone on the common,

beneath the lane of ruptured plane-trees.
There was our garden (we thought it ours),
wild with roses beside a holed water-tank,
no sign a donkey had tramped its weed-stilted paddock

except, cemented into the bricks, the iron ring.

The Age of Treason

i. The Clouds of History

Along the reedy sheets of quiet river,
the mottled swans have broken with their plumage.
Sullen and adolescent, they gnaw the tourist's pliant hand.
Fresh, disordered water laps the bank.

November's cold bonfires flare like a Géricault
under a lamplit sky. The electric ghosts gather,
huddled by towpaths overgrown with beech.
New faiths devour the water parliament.

Touch the wet stone and the stone flakes . . .

ii. Linnaeus and the Names of Adam

The dream a maze, in the maze nothing happens:
pocked whitewashed walls hunt down
the clipped hedgerow mired in horsehair plaster—
a nightmare, of course, but when does it run its course?
Death's coach and four, the horses whinnying
in scrape and sunflash of the blooming plum.
Linnaeus plucked Greek myth and made it whole—
Patroclus, decked in another's armor, his youthful hand
holding the shaking spear of middle age.

iii. The Doppelgänger

Europe's magpie, beak stuffed with treaties,
reverent debate, struts over the Queen's derelict estate.
Even history fingers a music lost to Handel's ear,

destiny stopped in the uncaught note.
Each oak sheaf gouged by Gibbons stalls the hour.
A ghostly figure shivers out of focus,

invisible against the papered wall, the one guest
who can never refuse a blazing invitation. The flesh
owes its debt to one who cares coldly for flesh.

Floods in Cambridge

The water meadows slumped knee-deep,
as if someone had left on the tap.
A scow, or what looked like a scowl,

bobbed level with the common—
the river had finally risen to meet us.
A man plunged his bike down a path

that overnight had become a canal—
a true admiral, pedaling against the current.
We considered ourselves eighteenth century,

judging by what the eye could take,
as if every landscape were a mirror
of the Age of Reason.

Storm light shadowed the housetops,
the steaming, unruly, bulldog chimneys,
little Nelsons of defiance.

In every Turner, sunbursts scumbled the waters.
The evening looked
as if someone had struck a match across it.

The Expensive Dress

In the changing room
at Harvey Nichols, trapped
in a £460 sea-green Armani dress,
you stood, arms akimbo,

the frothy bias-cut confection
tangled at your waist.
You held your hands out, laughing.
I lifted the straps above your head,

while you slipped your breasts
into the binding cloth.
I was manhandling your skin again
into a skin perhaps even more beautiful

with you inside it. I had watched you
in a mirror at twenty-four,
naked and vulnerable,
the days before we had money.

In the department store,
you spun before the narrow glass,
the dress taking your curves,
even at fifty-two.

I had undressed you a hundred times,
though I had never dressed you before.
You shook your head.
It was not the dress for you.

The Jubilee! The Jubilee!

i.

It was a landscape full of itself: disfigured arches
that long ago might have been aqueducts,
a moss-covered canal or two, the local birds—
too few, really, to work up a philosophy.
The villages could muster a morris dancer on weekends
but not enough priests to guarantee a religion—
and yet the swan's nest had never been abandoned,
the politicians took only modest bribes,
and, if there were virgins, they were virgins
of a realistic kind. Of course, the view was nowhere
as grand as it once had been, but nothing
ever is, not when you have ambitions.
That was the country where we'd chosen to live,
though some have known it by a different name.

ii.

No one wondered where the kestrels had flown,
or why spies no longer visited. Frogs
were born spotless in disused filter-ponds.
Some nameless thing rustled through humid evenings,
an echo in a language once spoken
but now incomprehensible. If there were signs
or wonders, they were misunderstood.
Around the market, the council hung cheap bunting.
A sweating politician braced himself
and shouted to the crowd, beneath

a notorious bronze admiral raised on a plinth.
Peeling billboards advertised a possible future.
Some citizens were embarrassed by the famous victories,
but run-down houses still bore great names.

iii.

The yellow fenlands, blooming with rapeseed
became to the many a symbol of failure.
Beneath clouds forever almost unchanging,
black trains arrowed through untidy lots
past mirrored houses high-strung but unremarkable.
Occasionally a thunderhead built up
like a Corinthian column, or a thin hare juddered
across a naked field, fallow or not yet poisoned,
but never with a whisper of destiny.
Enough had been buried and forgotten,
except for the bruised crop-marks that revealed
ruined ditches, equivocal hedges, a betrayed villa.
Was it all just the coat of the sublime?
To watch the willows for a sign was unsound.

iv.

The klaxon bleating like an illness through the town
provided a shock of recognition,
and yet men went about their business
as if they'd been through all this before.

Bombs were still occasionally spaded up in the middens,
but lovers who lagged along the shingle
no longer spotted the concrete emplacements.
How long before even this view, unhappy as a rose,
would come to seem old fashioned?
Already brick walls in brown zones were choked with ivy.
Ditchdiggers of the old school wore jackets,
tugged their forelocks, said *ta* in shops.
The daffodils faltered; irises stood tattered as ghosts,
as long as it took to pay the deaths that were due.

v.

Eager though the men were to ingratiate themselves,
their faces betrayed a curious inadequacy
as they slipped out at dawn, or returned
through the rough light of evening.
Summer spilled carelessly down slate roofs.
How did they bear their heroic guilt?
Were they not aware of the late reports?
House martins nested under delicate eaves,
such precarious cliffs as the island made available,
and a long river silvered like a heavy French mirror,
the label on the back guaranteeing the *argenture*.
In any case the affair was long over,
if not entirely forgotten, for who could refuse
this little incarnation, this local martyrdom?

vi.

At the end of the road the great hall stood,
soon to be auctioned stone by stone,
but meanwhile stucco bungalows had improved
the magnificent prospect. The forecast had changed.
The village church's crumbling spire still
deserved mention in guidebooks; the rude
medieval wall paintings could be viewed
on alternate Tuesdays for a fee of two shillings.
Local blackbirds made an uncertain coordinate din.
When did they lose the tarry patience of Jerome?
The heavy air, the shade of a pearl-gray army
waiting for battle, or merely for orders to disperse,
hovered over tables laid for tea in the abandoned
orchard, not that anyone had appeared.

vii.

The obscure beetle hatched in the wood,
but its house was corrupt and could not endure.
No peace had been declared on the borders;
and unemployment, though no longer rising,
settled like a cloth over the foundry towns.
The preachers polished old sermons by changing
the seven deadly sins to *a heaven fed by gins*
and scratching out *the meek shall inherit the earth.*
Old hedges raised the motley of the magpie.
Tax collectors gathered on railway platforms,

while biographies were written of pop stars
and saints who underwent curious tortures.
The odor of must and damp rising from the floorboards,
marriages were common but few children were born.

viii.

Elsewhere, sun-stippled ponds bathed in moral grandeur
and midges fanned upward through the glow.
That was in a country we had learned not to mention.
In the smoke-clad fires of frost, iris petals
blurred the rotting trellis. A low army of slugs
shouldered its way through the leafy smoulder.
There was the world, and the world
beneath the world. In the plum-garnet evening,
the capital commissioned its own self-portrait.
Candled chandeliers had been hauled to the ceiling.
We could almost hear tides washing
across marble lobbies embedded with seashells.
What was the question? we might have asked,
if the weather had not answered it for us.

ix.

Heat burned from the margins to the center.
One after another, houses sprouted FOR SALE signs
under dignified, gunmetal Armani skies.
In those mortgage-mad, low-interest days,

the decade was still without a name, though some
had suggested the "double noughts."
Who lived in the vegetable world of English Heritage,
with its lapsed gardens and steaming houses?
The Queen suffered her jubilee like a god—
with a wax smile. Each filigree on her gold coach
caught the glare of Turner's lost sunsets.
What remained was a language spent of emotion.
How do we oil the machinery of grace? England,
O England! There would have been time, etc.

Christ Church, Spitalfields

Spirit, at ease! The costermongers hawk
their gods no more, Hawksmoor. The Ten Bells tolls

the opening hour for tourists dressed to kill.
They drain warm pints and shy at whitewashed whores.

A Christian church breathes a theology
of verticals—its rough spire drills at God;

but here the ghosts of the baroque still haunt
the barrel-vaulted aisle, the gallery front

bitten by worm, the beetle-riddled post.
The leaded windows flare with falling light;

the market doors are locked, the empty shell
working the air where flights of angels throng.

The gutted blockhouse of your parish church
takes the dead street-end like a Wellington.

The Blaschkas' Invertebrates

i.

Low tide. The Thames. The shattered foreshore. Noon.
Moss crawls among the rocks—the crackled glaze
of a Victorian teacup, broken pipestems,
ship's nails, a stoneware jug from the Dover Road,
a shard marked "——ition 1862,"
half a black brick embossed with the Star of David,
the ballast of the past's cold repertoire
binding the gloomy depths beyond the tides'
hell-dark, tarred, inconsequential reach.
The Styx has ebbed, at whose edge mortal souls
abandoned their gods—rinsed, dulled, weathered, oiled—
dredged now beyond the vantage of the tide,
the shore fern-green, the river dead, long dead,
though in Great-grandfather's day the muscled trout
swam upward to the fly, the moon-gray bream
fell gigged beneath the shade of Parliament.

The leaves burn green to gold, and gold to ash.
In a silk kimono with the ink of leaves
starred on her cream-white breasts, her taut waist bound
lubriciously in belts, her soft feet cased
in sandals, and a paper parasol
tossed carelessly across a fetching shoulder,
the woman stood before the bellowed camera
at the studio the Messrs. Downey kept
on Eaton Square. The fleeting images,
features exposed through a forgiving lens,
were fixed on paper cards, called cabinets.

After a morning spent in Castellani's shop,
the modest tea at Fortnum's, in the Savoy,
from a steaming box's velvet dark, she gazed
down on the floating world of *The Mikado*,
wearing the sterling brooch, the lifelike shell,
bought at her jeweler's on account, its folds
enclosing, like living flesh, the etcher's craft,
the molten sorceries of the silversmith.

ii.

Theirs was a country staffed with German kings.
Their century had given the age of craft
the arts of war—the rifled barrels blazing
along the deadly squares at Waterloo,
echoing down the trenches of the Somme,
the lightning rattle of well-greased Maxim guns,
apologetic cough of cannon fire.
Amor ex machina. Who has not seen
the savage turning of the watchwork gear
mimic a snowflake's diatomic glaze,
or in the curl of the chambered nautilus
the mathematician's formulaic curve?
How much was paid at last, must yet be paid,
for those refinements of exquisite taste,
that X-ray progress of mechanic souls;
and to what depths does artistry descend?
The leaves burn green to gold, and gold to ash,
rising like acid smoke above the dead.

In the chilled rooms at Auschwitz, where the Jews
undressed the Jews; dragged out the stifled corpses;
pawed the soiled bodies for gold jewelry
stubbed in vagina, tucked beneath a tongue;
screwed off gold rings; dug gold from carious teeth;
laid out on shelves kid shoes or spectacles;
posed artificial limbs, fine ropes of hair;
men thumbed against an ink-stained manifest
the blind accounting's double-entry columns—
and, in that special kind of love called order,
nothing was lost, nothing was ever lost
except the chamber's *Muss es sein? Es muss sein!*

One day, a gray-browed SS man appeared,
eyeing the shuffling line of new arrivals,
and saw, amid the steamy, shouldering mass,
halfway already to the deadly showers,
a jet-haired girl with gypsy in her eyes.
She was deloused, scrubbed clean with Belgian soap,
and led off to his quarters, where he took,
in coming weeks, and months, his time with her.
Tiring at last, he sent her to the guards,
who each night found ingenious uses for her
before they put a Luger to her ear.

To seize the floating world beyond the dust,
annealed in taste and polished for the eye,
the creatures of the sea, dust long corrupt,
lie glowing still, as if infused with light
or caught in the burning rain of Dante's hell.

iii.

The girl had been nineteen, convicted during the Cultural Revolution of an offense against the state, some stray remark scribbled in a love note to her boyfriend, who betrayed her. She spent ten years in jail, begging the authorities for a new trial. This was taken as evidence that she was incapable of reform. At her appeal, the judges condemned her to death. Dragged to the center of the sports stadium, she knelt before her executioners. An ambulance rattled up. Her arms were pinned, and doctors—if they *were* doctors—crouched to cut out her kidneys while she was still alive. The doctors—if they were doctors—had been ordered to administer no anaesthetic. Blood stained the prisoner's cotton trousers. When the kidneys had been packed in ice, a nervous young soldier shot the half-conscious girl in the back of the head. Her parents were charged some small sum for the fatal bullet. They were afraid to claim the body, so in the wastes outside the stadium it was dumped for the local dogs. That night a janitor raped the corpse, then cut out the dead girl's vagina as a souvenir. He kept it in a jar—like a purple tube-sponge. This is a story told by Yiyun Li.

iv.

Downriver, in high-ceilinged galleries,
the Blaschkas' glass invertebrates, the last
remnants of mad Bohemian enterprise,
gutter like candles in the shuttered rooms.
Glassblowers breathed such creatures into life—

jellyfish like upended chandeliers,
their pale, translucent flesh a glossy film;
a feathery starfish like an armature
of delicate fir branches; a leafy slug;
a sea anemone's pointillist chaos
cooling the pink infection of a troglodyte;
the pewter brooch of squid, eyes like black opals;
the moody slouch of pearl-gray octopus;
a ruddy sea slug like a baked potato;
a protozoan's jeweled, milk-white spines—
as if, into the black of Newton's zone,
a thousand flares had jetted from the sun.
Muss es sein? they whisper. *Es muss sein!*

Dawn Chorus

Long awake in the uncertain dark, you slip
beyond the dream or half dream
where the garden gate opens to the rip
of wind, the irritated rustle of stream.

Notes

Mocha Dick, whose grounds lay off the coast of Chile, was the white whale on which Melville based the tale of Moby Dick. This mottled or cream-colored leviathan, who was friendly until roused, had destructive encounters with whalers for some fifty years. He was at last killed in 1859.

Leopold and Rudolf Blaschka, Dresden glassmakers, were famous for the glass flowers they made between the 1880s and the 1930s. Their invertebrates are more beautiful and even more haunting.

Section 3 of "The Blaschkas' Invertebrates" is based on the article "What Has That to Do with Me?" by Yiyun Li, published in the *Gettysburg Review*, Summer 2003.

About the Author

William Logan has published eight volumes of poetry and four volumes of essays and reviews. *The Undiscovered Country* won the National Book Critics Circle Award in criticism. He lives in Gainesville, Florida, and Cambridge, England.

PENGUIN POETS